MVFOL

D0578473

OUR
BURDEN
OF
SHAME

OUR BURDEN OF SHAME

JAPANESE-AMERICAN INTERNMENT DURING WORLD WAR II

BY SUSAN SINNOTT

A First Book
Franklin Watts
New York / Chicago / London / Toronto / Sydney

The excerpt by Yoshiko Uchida is from *Journey to Topaz: A Story of the Japanese-American Evacuation* published by Scribner, ©1971, pp. 25–26, and the excerpt by Lili Sasaki is from *Beyond Words: Images from America's Concentration Camps* published by Cornell University Press, ©1987, p. 15.

Cover art by Jane Sterrett

Photographs copyright ©: The Miyatake Collection: p. 2; UPI/Bettmann: pp. 8, 10, 24, 25, 27, 28, 31, 34, 42, 44, 52, 54, 55; The Bettmann Archive: p. 13; North Wind Picture Archives: p. 15; Archive Photos: p. 16; Library of Congress: pp. 20, 37, 46; The National Archives: pp. 22, 40, 47, 50; Wide World Photos: p. 33.

Library of Congress Cataloging-in-Publication Data

Sinnott, Susan.
    Our burden of shame : Japanese-American internment during World War II / by Susan Sinnott.
        p. cm.— (A First book)
    Includes bibliographical references and index.
    ISBN 0-531-20194-5
    1. World War, 1939–1945—Japanese Americans—Juvenile literature. 2. Japanese Americans—Evacuation and relocation, 1942–1945—Juvenile literature. [1. Japanese Americans—Evacuation and relocation, 1942–1945. 2. World War, 1939–1945—United States.] I. Title. II. Series.
D769.8.A6S56 1995
940.53'1503956073—dc20

94-22492
CIP
AC

CONTENTS

AN IMPOSSIBLE IDEA

Ken thought that talk of an evacuation was more than a rumor, but Yuki couldn't believe him. How in the world could they ever gather up all the Japanese in California and shift them somewhere else? Where would they go? What would happen to all their homes? It was an impossible idea.

"You're crazy," she said to Ken.

But Ken said ominously, "You just wait. You'll see whether I'm crazy or not."

Yoshiko Uchida

It did sound crazy at first, not just to Yoshiko Uchida, her family, and the rest of the Japanese in California but to people of all races in every part of the United States. In early 1942, just a few months after the Japanese bombing of the U.S. naval base at Pearl Harbor, Hawaii, the idea of evacuating all the Japanese and Japanese-Americans from the West Coast and sending them to internment camps stunned even

After Japan's attack on Pearl Harbor in December 1941, anti-Japanese sentiment rose dangerously. Signs like this one, which appeared in a Boston restaurant, were not uncommon.

federal officials in Washington, D.C. On December 10, just three days after the bombing of Pearl Harbor, FBI director J. Edgar Hoover said the Japanese living on the West Coast did not pose enough of a security threat to warrant their mass evacuation. One congressman proclaimed, "Let us not make a mockery of our Bill of Rights by mistreating these folks."

It happened anyway. Why? There's a war on, the exclusionists said, and we can't take any chances. But in 1942 the United States was at war with Germany and Italy, too, and American citizens from those countries weren't being rounded up and sent in crowded trains to remote western deserts. With the help of hindsight, the real reason seems obvious: racism. After the bombing of Pearl Harbor, newspapers, especially in California, relaxed all standards of fairness as anti-Japanese hysteria became the rule of the day. "Herd 'em up, pack 'em off, and give 'em the inside room in the badlands," wrote a columnist for the Hearst newspapers. *The Los Angeles Times* called Japanese-Americans "vipers."

So, with public opinion leading the way, in February 1942 President Franklin D. Roosevelt ordered more than 110,000 *Issei* (those born in Japan who immigrated to the United States) and *Nisei* (their children who were American citizens) into relocation camps, where most were forced to stay until 1945. Forty years later, during hearings held before the Congressional Commission on Wartime Relocation and Internment of Civilians (CWRIC), many Japanese-Americans, urged on by younger family members, spoke of their wartime prison sentences for

UNITED STATES DEPARTMENT OF JUSTICE

★

NOTICE
TO ALIENS OF ENEMY
NATIONALITIES

★ The United States Government requires all aliens of German, Italian, or Japanese nationality to apply at post offices nearest to their place of residence for a Certificate of Identification. Applications must be filed between the period February 2 through February 7, 1942. *Go to your postmaster today for printed directions.*

EARL G. HARRISON,
Special Assistant to the Attorney General.

FRANCIS BIDDLE,
Attorney General.

AVVISO

Il Governo degli Stati Uniti ordina a tutti gli stranieri di nazionalità Tedesca, Italiana e Giapponese di fare richiesta all' Ufficio Postale più prossimo al loro luogo di residenza per ottenere un Certificato d'Identità. Le richieste devono essere fatte entro il periodo che decorre tra il 2 Febbraio e il 7 Febbraio 1942.

Andate oggi dal vostro Capo d'Ufficio Postale (Postmaster) per ricevere le istruzioni scritte.

BEKANNTMACHUNG

Die Regierung der Vereinigten Staaten von Amerika fordert alle Auslaender deutscher, italienischer und japanischer Staatsangehoerigkeit auf, sich auf das ihrem Wohnorte naheliegende Postamt zu begeben, um einen Personalausweis zu beantragen. Das Gesuch muss zwischen dem 2. und 7. Februar 1942 eingereicht werden.

Gehen Sie noch heute zu Ihrem Postmeister und verschaffen Sie sich die gedruckten Vorschriften.

敵國外人注意

日獨伊諸國國籍ヲ有スル在雷外人ハ二月二日ヨリ七日マデノ間ニ其居所ニ番近イ郵便局デ自分證明書ヲ申シ込ム可シ。會モ早速郵便局ヘ行キテ説明書ヲ頼様ニ願ヒマス、

Post This Side in States of
Arizona, California, Idaho, Montana, Nevada, Oregon, Utah, Washington

the first time. They felt both sorrow and relief as they broke their long silence and finally found the words to describe their suffering.

> I don't think you can actually tell people how awful it was at that time, how terrible it was. And how embarrassing, because we thought we were being such good citizens and everything. It was a terrible state to be in, really. It was awful. Yes it was. We didn't know what to do.
>
> Lili Sasaki

In 1988, the commission concluded that the imprisonment of Japanese-Americans during World War II had been unjustified. Furthermore, they found that the decision to evacuate was based on "race prejudice, war hysteria, and a failure of political leadership." That same year the U.S. Congress passed a bill that officially apologized to American citizens of Japanese ancestry and gave a payment of twenty thousand dollars to each survivor of the detention camps. President Ronald Reagan signed the bill into law, calling it time to end "a sad chapter in American history."

In early 1942, the U.S. government attempted to identify all noncitizens from Italy, Germany, and Japan. By the end of the month officials decided the West Coast Japanese—citizens and noncitizens alike—posed enough of a threat to warrant internment.

THE BRIEF HISTORY OF THE JAPANESE IN AMERICA

Japan, like its Asian neighbor China, has spent long periods of its history out of the view of the rest of the world. These periods of isolation have seemed necessary to various autocratic rulers as a way of assuring national and ethnic purity. In 1637 the shogunate—a kind of military dictatorship—of the powerful Japanese Tokugawa family seized control from the ruling emperor and, for all intents and purposes, removed Japan from the international scene. Two hundred years later, in 1853, after internal fighting had finally weakened the Tokugawa's hold on the country, Commodore Matthew Perry of the U.S. Navy sailed his ship into Tokyo Bay. He returned in 1854 to sign a treaty that brought Japan back into the world community.

In 1867, after years of violent struggle, the forces of

Commodore Matthew C. Perry (1794–1858) who
in 1853 sailed into Tokyo Bay and ended Japan's
200-year isolation from the rest of the world

Emperor Meiji won out over the feudal power of the Tokugawa Shogunate. The Meiji era saw the beginning of a modern Japan, whose economy began to move quickly away from its centuries-old agricultural base. The new emperor and his officers saw the immense possibilities of international trade and began abruptly shifting workers into industrial jobs. By any measure their success was astonishing: by 1900 Japan had become both an economic and military world power.

Such a dramatic change in a nation's economy doesn't come without a price, however. Before the beginning of the Meiji era, the lives of the average Japanese had been virtually unchanged for two hundred years. Most lived on small family farms, where they grew rice, which they sold to the government, and perhaps raised a few chickens. While many ambitious Japanese men welcomed the opportunity to work in industry or be drafted into the military, others resisted any change and clung to the old ways of the shogunate. The result was that whole areas of Japan, especially in the South, became impoverished as many farmers insisted on growing rice in the time-honored tradition while large, modern, government-supported farms produced this staple more efficiently elsewhere.

Because there was no social safety net, when demand for the small farmer's rice disappeared, they and their families faced terrible hardship. When word spread, therefore, throughout southern Japan that farm labor was badly needed both in Hawaii and California, husbands, fathers, and sons began to cross the Pacific to earn a liv-

**By 1880 California's anti-Chinese emigration
laws had slowed the arrival of new
farmworkers from China. Eventually, grape
growers turned to Japanese laborers instead.**

ing wage. By the late 1860s the sugar plantations on the
Hawaiian Islands were in full production and looking for
ever more workers. By the 1880s, anti-Chinese legisla-
tion in California had effectively stopped new emigration
from China. So, when the Japanese expressed a desire
to fill badly needed farm jobs, the response was posi-
tive—at first, anyway.

The Japanese men who made the long, arduous journey across the sea hated leaving their homes and families. Their solace, however, was in knowing they were contributing to their very survival. According to traditional Japanese values, bringing honor to one's family was a lofty goal, so these men were willing to sacrifice their personal happiness.

The gains, to be sure, were great. By 1886, when unrestricted emigration from Japan was finally possible, monthly wages were fourteen dollars in California and only two dollars in Japan. At the same time, rural sections of southern Japan continued their steady decline into deep poverty, and the number of farmers forced to look for work in the United States grew. In 1890, U.S. Census figures reported the number of Japanese—mostly young men—living here at 2,039. By 1900 the figure was nearly 25,000. Many of these workers held out the hope of one day returning to Japan, but as the years went by and families grew ever more reliant on the high American wages, these men themselves resigned to never seeing their homeland again.

The Japanese government, however, unlike that of China or the governments in Europe, took some interest in its emigrants. Part of its concern was to protect citizens

Agricultural workers from poverty-stricken southern Japan were eager to earn high wages on Hawaii's sugar plantations or California's fruit farms.

from inevitable white racist sentiments. The Japanese understood the plight of the Chinese, who had worked hard at jobs no one else wanted and, for their trouble, were relegated to overcrowded, squalid Chinatowns. Japan paid close attention to the conduct of its citizens abroad, and tried to make sure they held up the honor of their country. The government bought western clothing for the workers so they wouldn't stand out too much—as the Chinese had with their baggy "pajamas" and long pigtails called queues. The Japanese also gave their emigrants money so their poverty wouldn't call attention to itself.

This concern with appearances backfired, however, as anti-Asian propagandists saw in it evidence that Japan, far from trying to help its citizens, was simply using them to take over the western United States. By the early 1890s these exclusionists, as they were called, began to spread the word that, contrary to what had been expected, the Japanese were no different from the Chinese. The forces organized for the cause of preventing Chinese emigration, which had successfully passed an exclusion act in 1882, quickly turned their attention to the Japanese. White politicians interested in quick political gain had only to appeal to the most basic fears of the average American worker—that Asians would take over not only their livelihoods but their very way of life as well—to see their fortunes rise. Many wasted no time or energy in spreading their venal message.

"Separate but not equal" became the rallying cry for anti-Asian forces throughout California. By the early 1900s, Asians were allowed to attend school only with other Asians—Chinese, Koreans, Japanese, or Filipinos. Everywhere there were worrying signs that Asians were becoming dangerously isolated from American society. When the anti-Japanese forces began holding demonstrations throughout California, no one was surprised when they took a violent turn.

Despite these protests and the growing risks to the Japanese, emigration continued. In 1924, however, President Calvin Coolidge added the Japanese to the list of Asians who were specifically denied the right to become U.S. citizens. From that year emigration from Japan slowed drastically.

As with the Chinese, the fact that the Japanese were doing necessary jobs that others didn't want to do did not dissuade the exclusionists. Still, for all the fear and criticism, the Japanese had rarely competed directly with whites. Instead they worked in the only areas open to them. During the first wave of emigration, the Japanese had worked mainly on sugar plantations and fruit farms in California. They proved themselves, much to the frustration of their detractors, to be both industrious and skilled at business.

A few Japanese had even worked and saved enough to buy their own farms, news of which brought not praise but panic from Californians. The number of Japanese-owned farms declined after the 1924 exclusion law went into effect, however. The Japanese had enriched themselves by growing so-called specialty crops—artichokes, strawberries, cantaloupes, for example—that yielded a high profit. Japanese growers were also important to

Japanese farm families in
California in the early 1900s

California's flower industry. And again, the more success they achieved, the more exclusionists began to think it was time to turn them away from our shores.

Despite the Asian exclusion laws, the threat of the Yellow Peril (the feeling among Americans that Asians wouldn't be satisfied until they'd taken over all of the U.S. mainland) continued to grow. The very large exclusionist forces clung determinedly to the idea that Japanese immigration was part of a secret plot. Outlandish stories were told about how Japanese fruit growers were spreading contaminated fertilizer on their crops so that white Americans would be infected with deadly diseases. Another persistent story held that a Japanese-owned fishing fleet was hiding off the coast of northern California, transforming its trawlers into torpedo boats. The fishers, this rumor held, were really officers in the Japanese Navy. Newspaper reports maintained that this fleet of more than 2,000 fishers was preparing to supply the more than 500,000 heavily armed Japanese already living on the West Coast. In 1935, however, the United States government itself could count only 135,000 Japanese in the three Pacific states and only 680 licensed Japanese fishers. They looked and looked for the "fleet" but only managed to track down two boats that were actually Japanese owned.

That the Japanese imperialist forces in Asia were acting aggressively on that continent could certainly not be denied, however. When Japan invaded China in the 1930s, Americans living on the West Coast became increasingly nervous and the anti-Japanese political forces sounded

The Japanese were forced to sell everything as they prepared for relocation. Many Japanese-American fishermen had saved for years to buy their own boats and were distraught to have to give them up.

even more shrill. When the Japanese Navy attacked the U.S. naval base at Pearl Harbor in Hawaii on December 7, 1941, the exclusionists were suddenly joined by normally rational citizens in thinking there might be something to this talk of Yellow Peril after all.

PEARL HARBOR

When the Japanese staged their surprise air attack on the U.S. naval base at Pearl Harbor, Hawaii, any hope that the Issei and Nisei might have had of being accepted as true Americans faded away. The militaristic ambitions of Japan left her former sons and daughters virtually stranded. Most Japanese-Americans had no interest in supporting Japan's totalitarian regime yet they found themselves objects of scorn in the United States.

They had hoped it wouldn't be so. At first they had believed Americans might see them as fellow patriots, concerned above all with their new homeland. After all, hadn't 2,000 Japanese-American soldiers fought in the defense of America at Pearl Harbor? In the eyes of these citizens, Japan had attacked *their* country, too.

Rumors about the possibility of relocation camps for the Issei and Nisei living along the West Coast began almost before the last Japanese plane sped away from Pearl Harbor. Some people in the federal government in Washington, D.C., however, maintained for several weeks that interning the Japanese along the West Coast was both unnecessary and unwise. On December 8, just one day after the attack, Congressman John Coffee declared on the floor of the House of Representatives, "It is my fervent hope and prayer that residents of the United States of Japanese extraction will not be made the victims of programs directed by self-proclaimed patriots.... Let us rather regard them with understanding, remembering they are the victims of a Japanese war machine."

Representative John M. Coffee of Washington spoke on behalf of Japanese-Americans.

There was some basis for Congressman Coffee's optimism. One month before Pearl Harbor, President Franklin Roosevelt had commissioned a secret report on the matter of Japanese-American loyalty. This report, written by a Chicago businessman named Curtis Munson, discounted the fear that the Japanese population would ever engage in espionage or sabotage. "For the most part," he concluded, "the local Japanese are loyal to the United States or, at worst, hope that by remaining quiet they can avoid concentration camps or irresponsible mobs. We do not believe that they would be at least any more disloyal than any other racial group in the U.S. with whom we went to war."

By January 1942, however, the press and public, especially in California, were clearly in no frame of mind to heed the calm, reasoned words of Congressman Coffee or Curtis Munson. The press campaigned particularly hard. "I am for immediate removal of every Japanese on the West Coast to a point deep in the interior. I don't mean a nice part of the interior either," wrote one Hearst newspaper columnist. The well-respected columnist Walter Lippmann wrote more elegantly, if no less pointedly, in *The Washington Post*, as he called for the removal of all Japanese-Americans from the West Coast, "The Pacific Coast is officially a combat zone . . . and nobody ought to be on a battlefield who has no good reason for being there."

**Newspaper columnist
Walter Lippmann**

As the press became more outspoken, patriotic organizations such as the American Legion and California groups such as Native Sons and Daughters of the Golden West, pressed what they, too, saw as the just cause. The solution was simple, they said: concentration camps. These groups lashed out particularly hard at the Nisei, who were American citizens. Far from feeling that fellow citizens deserved full protection under the U.S. Constitution, the so-called patriotic groups saw the American-born Japanese as even more dangerous than the first-generation Issei. They saw no contradiction in the position that while they promoted the glories of American democracy, they pushed for the incarceration of fellow citizens without due cause. At first, most politicians reacted cautiously to the idea of relocating the Japanese into massive prison camps. When they saw, however, the fervor of public opinion following Pearl Harbor, nearly all jumped on the anti-Japanese bandwagon as well.

Lt. Gen. John L. DeWitt, head of the Western Defense Command, was in a position to study closely the evidence of a Japanese threat. While his counterpart in Hawaii saw no reason to suspect unreasonably the large Japanese populations on the islands, General DeWitt passionately made the case that Japanese disloyalty on the West Coast needed to be assumed, despite the few facts supporting this view. In early January, he asked for a meeting of federal and state officials and made the argument that military necessity warranted Japanese internment. In making this case, he completely ignored the Munson report, information from the FBI, as well as army officials who also found no cause for undue concern. Some openly dismissed DeWitt's actions as hysteria or a simple bowing to public and political pressure, but he could not be undone.

Still, the decision to evacuate the Japanese living along the Pacific Coast had to come from Washington, D.C. Secretary of War Henry L. Stimson wrote that he worried about the connection between mass evacuation and racism—weren't the two very closely linked? He believed such an order would "make a tremendous hole in our own constitutional system to apply it."

President Roosevelt, on the other hand, had thought about evacuating the Japanese long before Pearl Harbor. Afterward, he was ready to translate "military necessity" very loosely. Not sur-

**Secretary of War
Henry L. Stimson**

prisingly General DeWitt contacted Secretary Stimson and spoke to the issue of "necessity": "The Japanese race is an enemy race and while many second and third generation Japanese born on U.S. soil, possessed of U.S. citizenship, have become 'Americanized,' the racial strains are undiluted."

Attorney General Francis Biddle opposed evacuation and tried to speak to Secretary Stimson about the U.S. Constitution and the importance of preserving its integrity. His point was simple: someone had to demonstrate the

**Attorney General
Francis Biddle**

necessity of interning citizens and no one had the evidence to support it. But Congressional leaders, sensing that the public was ready to turn on its Japanese countrymen, threatened to debate the issue on the floor of the House and Senate, where, given the war-charged atmosphere, "discussion" would be politically devastating for the president's administration.

On February 19, President Roosevelt signed Executive Order 9066. The document was full of legal language that simply talked about prescribed military areas and "right to enter" and made no mention of the order's true purpose: It was a blank check, handed to General DeWitt, to define "necessity" according to his own judgment and prejudices.

Executive Order 9066 forced Japanese-Americans to evacuate the West Coast, a so-called "military area." The order was signed by President Roosevelt early in 1942.

EXECUTIVE ORDER

- - - - - - -

AUTHORIZING THE SECRETARY OF WAR TO PRESCRIBE
MILITARY AREAS

WHEREAS the successful prosecution of the war
requires every possible protection against espionage
and against sabotage to national-defense material,
national-defense premises, and national-defense util-
ities as defined in Section 4, Act of April 20, 1918,
40 Stat. 533, as amended by the Act of November 30,
1940, 54 Stat. 1220, and the Act of August 21, 1941,
55 Stat. 655 (U. S. C., Title 50, Sec. 104):

NOW, THEREFORE, by virtue of the authority
vested in me as President of the United States, and
Commander in Chief of the Army and Navy, I hereby
authorize and direct the Secretary of War, and the
Military Commanders whom he may from time to time
designate, whenever he or any designated Commander
deems such action necessary or desirable, to prescribe
military areas in such places and of such extent as he
or the appropriate Military Commander may determine,
from which any or all persons may be excluded, and with
respect to which, the right of any person to enter, remain in, or leave shall be subject to whatever restric-
tions the Secretary of War or the appropriate Military

EVACUATION

General DeWitt set about preparing to evacuate the Japanese from the West Coast with, as Yoshiko Uchida put it, "undisguised enthusiasm." The first group to be forced to leave their homes were residents of a small fishing village called Terminal Island near San Pedro, California. If their treatment at the hands of eager federal authorities was to be a guide, Japanese fears for their future well-being were not without reason.

The closeness of Terminal Island to a naval base was the official explanation for the speed of this first evacuation. The families, most now headed by women because the men had been imprisoned just after Pearl Harbor, were given just three days to vacate their homes completely. Needless to say, they suffered both great personal and financial losses as they scrambled frantically to sell or store all personal belongings.

After the signing of Executive Order 9066, Terminal
Island was placed under the jurisdiction of the U.S.
Navy. Japanese-American residents were served
papers that ordered them to leave within three days.

As other Japanese along the West Coast waited for their evacuation notices, they were placed under a 5-mile (3-km) travel restriction and an 8 P.M. curfew. When the notice to vacate finally did come, it was usually with a ten-day deadline. Yoshiko Uchida's family read about their evacuation orders in a local Berkeley, California, newspaper. "Japs Given Evacuation Orders Here!" the headlines read on April 21, 1942. They and 1,300 others in the area frantically began to dispose of a lifetime's accumulation of furniture, clothing, books, and personal items such as scrapbooks and papers that couldn't be taken into the camps.

All evacuees needed to bring, the newspaper notices told them, were bedding, some clothing, and toilet articles. Because they could bring so little, families that rented houses or apartments needed to either store their belongings or get rid of them. Those evacuees who owned their homes could risk leaving their belongings inside them, although they worried—and with good reason—that there would be nothing left when they returned.

Pets were not permitted in the camps and one of the saddest aspects of the evacuation was the number of dogs and cats that had to be given up. For Yoshiko Uchida's family, deciding what to do with their old collie, Laddie, caused them particular grief. Yoshiko put an ad in the University of California student newspaper and was able to give Laddie to a young man who promised to give him a new home. The new owner promised, too, to write them news of Laddie, but they never heard from him. When they finally asked a friend to looked into the mat-

As a military policeman stands guard, a young boy waits for the return of his parents. The family from San Francisco had just arrived at the Santa Anita Assembly Center near Los Angeles.

As they await processing, evacuees are crowded into barracks. Since the assembly centers were often under construction, delays could be long and agonizing.

ter, they discovered that Laddie had died shortly after leaving the Uchidas and the student simply hadn't had the heart to tell them.

After the heart-wrenching experience of leaving their homes, the evacuees reported to control centers where each person registered and was given a tag with a number on it. Later, wearing their tags around their necks, they were taken to train stations where, surrounded by soldiers with rifles and fixed bayonets, they were herded onto trains bound for assembly centers. The "assembly centers," it turned out, were nothing more than holding areas. The executive order to evacuate had been given so quickly, the relocation camps couldn't be readied nearly fast enough, so temporary quarters needed to be found. Up and down the West Coast former racetracks, stockyards, and fair grounds, such as the Tanforan racetrack near San Francisco, where the Uchidas went, were quickly converted into barracks.

None of the Japanese were quite prepared when they caught sight of what would be their new "homes." First there were the high barbed-wire fences with tall guard towers at regular intervals. Everywhere there were armed soldiers wearing heavily the responsibility of their shoot-to-kill orders. Then there were the crowds, which were noisy and chaotic as the nearly 8,000 people in any one assembly center set about trying to live one next to the other.

Finally, there was the realization that their new family living quarters were nothing more than converted horse stalls that had only tarpaper-covered boards to separate them from their neighbors. Their rooms were nothing more than patched-up animal stalls, which had been hurriedly converted into housing. Whole families were to stay in dark, poorly ventilated spaces that were no more than 10 feet (33 m) by 20 feet (65 m). Bedding consisted of gunny sacks filled with straw laid out on linoleum that had been put over manure-covered floorboards. Everywhere there was dust and dirt and the smell of horses.

Many evacuees remembered above all the lack of privacy and the noise. The knotty wood used to build the animal stalls couldn't keep out the eyes or ears of nosy neighbors. Sleeping often seemed impossible as the talking, coughing, and snoring of thousands of "roommates" continued until dawn. "You could hear all the people crying, the people grinding their teeth; you could hear everything."

During the day there were lines for everything—for meals, mail, toilets, showers, and laundry. And if the lines themselves weren't bad enough, there was always a rush to get from one to the other. Meals were scheduled much earlier than anyone was used to, and the food, at first, was skimpy and of poor quality. Days would go by without the sight of a fresh vegetable or fruit in any form. There was always bread and beans and sometimes canned corn. When a small lettuce salad would miraculously appear for lunch or dinner, evacuees would savor the leafy greens as though they were the rarest delicacies.

The stay at the assembly centers was, however, brief. By mid-summer 1942, rumors began to circulate that the evacuees might soon head inland—to the camps

As a train arrives at an internment camp,
new residents are greeted by the fixed
bayonets of the military guard.

that would become their more permanent homes. By this time though, most internees had done what was necessary to make the assembly centers as pleasant as possible. Gardens had been planted along the barracks and stables. Besides giving evacuees the fresh produce they badly needed, the zinnias and marigolds and sweetpeas added color to this otherwise drab life.

Still, there was a sense of relief, as well as anxiety, at knowing that the next journey—the real journey—was at hand. For many there were several days of anxious waiting as train after train filled with passengers and headed east into the unknown. Each train carried five hundred evacuees and because thousands needed to be sent off to the newly completed relocation camps, the wait could be very long. As the night trains pulled away from the assembly centers, there was much waving and shouting good-bye to both new and old friends.

As the trains streamed east to what were to the evacuees completely unknown locations, many seemed to realize for the first time that these crowded, noisy cars were taking them to prison. Many people, especially the old ones, sank into depressed silence. As the train sped through the snowy mountain passes and into sagebrush country, passengers pulled photographs from their pockets. These pictures were of themselves, their children, homes, pets. They would look long and lovingly at these pictures. It seemed as though they believed that even if they had no idea where they were going, they could at least remember who they were and where they'd come from.

CAMP
LIFE

After a wearying journey of several days, the trains finally arrived at their destinations. There were ten different internment camps scattered throughout remote sections of the West. Their names now seem tinged with tragedy: Topaz in Utah, Poston and Gila River in Arizona, Amache in Colorado, Jerome and Rohuid in Arkansas, Minidoka in Idaho, Manzanar and Tule Lake in California, and Heart Mountain in Wyoming.

Although the names and states were different, the sites were quite similar. Most were in remote desert wastelands. There was nothing on the horizon, no trees, only sagebrush, dry earth, dust, and sand. "Sand filled our mouths and nostrils and stung our faces and hands like a thousand darting needles," remembered one evacuee.

The new arrivals, while still frightened and unnerved

**Dust storms were common in
the desolate internment camps.**

by their situation, were nonetheless now used to having
orders barked at them. They were taken to their barracks,
where each family was assigned a room which, while still
a pitifully small space for an entire family, was half again
as large as the quarters at the assembly centers. In each
room were a pot-bellied stove, army cots, blankets, and

a single electric light bulb hanging from the ceiling. They were dismayed, although not surprised, to see that construction had again been hasty and incomplete. It was several more weeks before crews arrived with sheetrock for the walls and ceiling.

Living in the internment camps was in many ways similar to being in the military, only this was an army not just of able-bodied young men, but of grandparents, mothers, and children, too. A siren blast at 7 A.M. was the signal to begin cleaning one's room and speed off for breakfast at the cafeteria. At first it seemed, once again, that the rushing was for its own sake; it filled the day. What were they rushing for? many wondered. Only to eat food covered with dust and sand.

At first, for residents at all the camps, the weather and desolation seemed intolerable. There was nothing to see, only sandstorms and tumbleweeds; and there was certainly nothing to do. Boredom and depression set in quickly. As Yoshiko Uchida wrote of Topaz, Utah, it was "as bleak as bleached bone."

There was nothing to see, that is, except the fence, the inevitable barbed wire that rimmed the camp. The War Relocation Authority had decided that each camp should be enclosed and guarded by sentry towers. As if, the residents scoffed, the desert and mountains weren't already enough of a barrier. The evacuees resented this fence more than anything else, except perhaps being incarcerated in the first place. "It seems to be mocking us in our faces," wrote one resident. The fence looked especially cruel in the early evening, after the hot sun had

A young child clings to his mother as she goes
through the cafeteria line of a camp mess hall.

set and the desert heat abated, and couples and families could enjoy a walk to view the brilliant sunset. Instead, it seemed, everywhere they looked they saw the fence.

After the first first few weeks, however, the inevitable inconveniences, such as the lack of hot water, long food lines, barracks that were either too hot or too cold, began to end. Now the Japanese again proved themselves to be very resourceful. They scavenged from the huge piles of scrap wood left over from camp construction what they needed to make furniture and everyday objects. Soon, too, camp residents were not only tilling the desert sand to make gardens, but they were organizing schools for children and clubs and classes for adults.

Something, of course, had to be done about the children's education, and so an Education Section was opened for each camp. These were headed by white Americans, although many residents, who'd been teachers in their pre-war lives, were also hired. Still, not surprisingly, the schools got off to a shaky start. As the newly hired teachers discovered on their first day of work, there were no table or chairs, light bulbs, or equipment of any kind. Some buildings hadn't been touched, and where pipes had been installed, gaping holes could be seen in the walls and ceiling. As the desert winds blew, sand and dust gathered everywhere.

Still, children flocked to these ill-equipped schools. They needed something to do and a chance to be away from their families with whom they lived so closely. Even in the first winter of 1942–1943, when snow fell and fin-

A young woman decorates the barrack room she shares with her husband. All the furniture was made by the couple from scrap lumber.

gers and toes ached from the cold, they came. For every-one—students, teachers, and staff—the schools meant a stability they couldn't find anywhere else.

Camp life was also made more bearable by packages and visitors from the outside. Many Japanese relied on food baskets given by former neighbors or friends or church groups to break the monotony of camp life. By 1943, spurred on by educational and religious associa-tions, opportunities for either employment or to attend school came through. Those Japanese-Americans inter-ested in attending colleges and universities away from the West Coast were given the chance. The National Japanese-American Student Relocation Council helped some 3,000 young people leave the camp for more than 500 different schools.

Despite the bright points, there was inevitable ten-sion and conflict as people facing very uncertain futures lived too close to one another. Not surprisingly, this some-times brought out the worst in people as rudeness and fighting became common. The older Japanese, the Issei, were especially distraught as they watched the traditional family values they held dear all but vanish.

All camp residents were stunned when on June 28, 1943, U.S. Secretary of War Henry Stimson announced a change in policy that would affect Japanese-Americans. The army would henceforth accept the Nisei as recruits. They intended, in fact, to create an all-Japanese combat team, a fact that only added to the turmoil and division among the camp inmates. Some were happy to volunteer to prove their loyalty. Others felt they couldn't fight for

A Girl Scout troop marches through one of the camps. It was especially important to school-age children that life seem as normal as possible.

their country because it had so little respect for their own rights.

Everyone, it seemed, was united in their disgust over one of the questions asked during the War Relocation Authority's mass registration of all camp residents, which

A U.S. serviceman visits his parents in their camp barracks. Even though they were often recruited directly from the camps, Japanese-American soldiers were among the most decorated of the war.

was being carried out at the same time as the army's recruitment of Nisei soldiers. Both questionnaires asked: "Will you swear any unqualified allegiance to the U.S.A. and foreswear any form of allegiance or obedience to the Japanese Emperor or any other foreign government power?" This was an ill-considered attempt by the government to determine loyalty, but its effect on internees was devastating. Didn't the government see that if they answered "Yes," that, because they were being unfairly imprisoned by the United States, they would in effect be without a country?

The young men who did join the military left behind very distraught families. What, they wondered, would it be like to lose a loved one in battle while still living in a government-run concentration camp? Many, sadly, would soon find out.

As the months wore on, young people were given more and more opportunities to leave the camps. The Issei, those born in Japan, were given none. They stayed behind to organize camp councils and often fight among themselves about the war. A few did openly support Japan and harassed those they believed were going too far to accommodate whites. All internees, no matter what their national loyalties, tried hard not to be swallowed by bitterness and anger as the war dragged into 1944 and their fates remained uncertain.

THE
ORDEAL
ENDS

In December 1944, the U.S. government announced that on January 2, 1945, the internment camps would begin to close. The reason, simply stated, was that federal authorities had determined the security risk from Japanese-Americans was minimal and not worth the huge expense of maintaining the ten camps. The orders that followed the public announcement were written in the rigid language of the military: "The relocation of camp residents would begin immediately and be completed by the end of 1945."

Despite the disgust Japanese-Americans felt at having spent years confined in the makeshift, desolate internment camps, this news was greeted not with joy but with general disbelief and worry. The long ordeal, the evacuees knew, wasn't really ending, just moving into a new phase.

By the time the government closed the camps in 1945, many residents had already resettled. The last to leave often feared the challenges of life on the outside.

There was not to be, they felt, a happy ending to their wartime story.

The reasons for their apprehension were easy to understand. When the evacuation orders were given in the spring of 1942, many had been forced to sell or give up their homes and personal belongings. During that confused, rushed period of evacuation, many Japanese were victims of those eager to take advantage of their misfortune. When they tried to sell their property, they were given criminally low prices. Those who decided to leave belongings behind, either locked in their homes or in storage centers, knew there was the very real possibility that everything would be either destroyed or confiscated.

Many, of course, had left jobs and businesses and now faced very uncertain employment prospects. Most Japanese-Americans felt certain, too, that popular feelings against them would be just as strong as before the war. They would face, they knew, ethnic discrimination and racial hostility. As the war raged on, those who had always opposed the presence of the Japanese found ample support from other citizens, especially on the West Coast. There seemed to be no reason now to hope for compassion.

Despite the difficulties of starting new lives during wartime, many Japanese-Americans had in fact already left their camps and resettled away from the West Coast. Early in the relocation process, there had been three kinds of camp leave available to residents. The first was short-term leave, for either medical or personal business, which was available only after very careful consideration by federal authorities. The next was seasonal leave, which allowed many to help with agricultural work. The third, and most difficult to obtain, was the so-called indefinite leave. To move away from the camp altogether, internees needed to prove they had some means of support, were not a threat to national security, and that their presence was acceptable to their new community. These three conditions were often very hard to prove and made the process excruciatingly slow.

To speed up the granting of indefinite leaves, the War

Many camp residents obtained leave to help with agricultural work. Here workmen build wooden beds to cultivate the guayule shrub, which is used to make synthetic rubber.

Relocation Authority opened field offices, which were intended to help the Japanese find work in "acceptable communities." ("Acceptable" meant those that would take the Japanese.) The first such office was opened in Chicago in January 1943.

To be sure, however, most Japanese-Americans

wanted to resettle in the familiar climate and surroundings of the West Coast. The harsh fact, however, was that many residents of California, Oregon, and Washington didn't want them. The midwestern states, however, and eventually the mid-Atlantic area, too, were unfazed by the presence of the Japanese. By 1945, there were eighteen thousand settled in the states of Illinois, Indiana, Wisconsin, and Minnesota, with twelve thousand in Chicago alone. Some farmed, but most found jobs in small businesses, which were eager to use the Japanese-Americans' skills.

Still, when the announcement was made that the camps would be closed, there were nearly eighty thousand internees, many of them the elderly Issei. The community councils at the individual camps lobbied to ensure that these people would not be resettled without adequate preparation. They stressed that speedy relocation would cause emotional hardship for a group of people who had already suffered enough. Besides the financial losses and prejudices, the Issei, who were mostly in their sixties, were dependent on sons who were off fighting in Europe. These older, more traditional Japanese were simply not up to the task of resettling without the guidance of their oldest male children.

Despite the difficulties, however, most internees had moved out of the camps by July 1945. By December the camps were completely deserted. As the Japanese began the long process of relocation and resettlement, there were some hopeful signs that America's attitude toward them had changed somewhat. Certainly, as the news spread of the brave Nisei soldiers of the 442nd

Camp residents at Manzanar in California were given the right to self-government. Here, the elected officials meet to decide camp policy.

Battalion, which President Harry Truman called "one of the most decorated units in military history," many openly expressed admiration for these men. This all-Japanese unit, most of whom had entered the army from the internment camps, earned 18,143 individual decorations, including more than 3,600 Purple Hearts. Many Am-

**Evacuees knew life outside the camp would be diffi-
cult. Here, five tenant farmers have just been forced
off a farm after neighbors protested their presence.**

ericans, even those who had urged Japanese internment,
couldn't help but admit this was an unequaled show of
patriotism and dedication.

Also, as former camp residents returned to the West
Coast, they found there were new groups, either Asian
Americans or others, willing to offer support. All in all

about half the total number of camp residents—about sixty thousand—returned to the Pacific Coast states. Significantly, this group was largely Issei, who were too old to look for employment.

Despite signs of support and optimism, those who did make it back to their homes on the West Coast were usually greeted with shocking proof that their lives would never be the same. Some found homes damaged or ransacked and personal belongings missing. One particularly sad case was that of the young writer Toshio Mori, who in the late 1930s had been praised by literary critics as a true talent. When he returned to his family's home and plant nursery in San Leandro, California—where he'd hurriedly stored his handwritten manuscripts in 1942—he found the paper had been eaten by bookworms. While Mori did continue writing, his career never quite recovered from this devastating setback.

In 1952, however, one dream did come true for the Japanese. After intense lobbying by the Japanese-American Citizen's League, the McCarran-Walter Act passed, finally making all Issei eligible for citizenship, a right previously denied them by the harsh Asian exclusion laws. Now, after long suffering the indignation of being considered "enemy aliens"—when, in fact, they'd never been eligible for citizenship in the first place—the Issei rejoiced in this victory for equality. By 1960 nearly fifty thousand Issei had taken the oath to become citizens of the United States.

REDRESS

It's not for us today to pass judgment upon those who have made mistakes while engaged in that great struggle. Yet we must recognize that the internment of Japanese-Americans was just that, a mistake.

President Ronald Reagan
August 10, 1988

With President Reagan's signing of the redress bill more than forty-five years after the evacuation order, the Japanese-Americans were finally able to believe their long nightmare was over. Now they could let go of the unreasonable shame and guilt they carried with them. Now they could move forward with their lives.

It had taken gentle prodding by children and grandchildren to convince the elderly Issei to break their silence and speak openly about their internment. The younger generation rejected the idea that their parents should view their internment as a "burden of shame." They begged them to tell more details of camp life, even as the elders pleaded in their turn to be allowed to forget. As Tanuka Nehira told the commission, "I've kept quiet, hoping in due time we will be justly compensated and recognized for our years of patient effort by my passive attitude. I can reflect on my past years to conclude that it doesn't pay to remain silent."

The writer Yoshiko Uchida, who spent nearly two years in the camp at Topaz, Utah, felt that the words to tell the story couldn't come out until they were ready. The process of remembering the incarceration was simply too painful to rush. It simply, as she wrote, "took so many years for these words to find a home."

The bill that passed also struck all pending lawsuits off the books. There had been several that had challenged the constitutionality of the evacuation order, specifically the part dealing with "military necessity." When in 1942 the JACL told its members that the best way to help the country was to cooperate with the order, three men, filing three separate suits in three separate states, challenged this idea. Gordon Hirabayashi of Washington, Fred Korematsu of California, and Minoru Yasui of Oregon went to prison rather than go along with the notion that their internment was dictated by "military necessity." Their legal battles continued for nearly forty years, helping to finally uncover the truth that the evacuation orders were motivated by racial prejudice.

And so, when President Reagan signed the Civil Liberties Act of 1988 and apologized for the government's past mistakes, the Second World War was finally over for all Japanese-Americans.

 # FOR FURTHER READING

Nonfiction

Chin, Steven A. *When Justice Failed: The Fred Korematsu Story*. Austin, Tex.: Raintree Steck-Vaughn, 1993.

Katz, William Loren. *World War II to the New Frontier, 1940–1963*. Austin, Tex.: Raintree Steck-Vaughn, 1993.

Kitano, Harry. *Japanese Americans, Racism and Renewal*. New York: Orchard Books, 1990.

Leathers, Noel L. *The Japanese in America*. Minneapolis: Lerner, 1991.

McGowen, Tom. *Go for Broke: Japanese-Americans in World War II*. New York: Franklin Watts, 1995.

Stanley, Jerry. *I Am an American: A True Story of the Japanese Internment*. New York: Crown, 1994.

Takashima, Shizuye. *A Child in Prison Camp*. New York: Morrow, 1974.

Uchida, Yoshiko. *The Invisible Thread: An Autobiography*. Englewood Cliffs, N.J.: Messner, 1991.

Wright, David K. *A Multicultural Portrait of World War II*. New York: Marshall Cavendish, 1994.

Fiction

Banim, Lisa. *American Dreams*. New York: Silver Moon Press, 1993.

Means, Florence Crannell. *The Moved-Outers*. New York: Walker, 1992.

Mochizuki, Ken. *Baseball Saved Us*. New York: Lee & Low, 1993.

Uchida, Yoshiko. *The Bracelet*. New York: Philomel, 1993.

INDEX

ABOUT THE AUTHOR

Susan Sinnott began her publishing career as an editor for *Cricket*, a literary magazine for children. She later worked at the University of Wisconsin Press, where she managed and edited academic journals. Eventually, her own two children pulled her away from scholarly publishing and helped her rediscover the joys of reading and writing books for young people. Ms. Sinnott's books include *Extraordinary Hispanic Americans*, *Extraordinary Asian Pacific Americans*, *Chinese Railroad Workers*, and *Doing Our Part: American Women on the Home Front during World War II*. She lives in Portsmouth, New Hampshire, with her husband and children.